D0426799

DEL REY
NEW YORK

Stay safe online. Any website addresses listed in this book are correct at the time of going to print. However, Del Rey is not responsible for content hosted by third parties. Please be aware that online content can be subject to change and websites can contain content that is unsuitable for children. We advise that all children are supervised when using the internet. This publisher does not have any control over and does not assume any responsibility for author or third-party websites or their content.

ONLINE SAFETY FOR YOUNGER FANS
Spending time online is great fun! Here are a few simple rules to help younger fans stay safe and keep the internet a great place to spend time:
- Never give out your real name—don't use it as your username.
- Never give out any of your personal details.
- Never tell anybody which school you go to or how old you are.
- Never tell anybody your password except a parent or a guardian.
- Be aware that you must be 13 or over to create an account on many sites. Always check the site policy and ask a parent or guardian for permission before registering.
- Always tell a parent or guardian if something is worrying you.

Copyright © 2017 by Mojang AB and Mojang Synergies AB. MINECRAFT is a trademark or registered trademark of Mojang Synergies AB.

Published in the United States by Del Rey, an imprint of Random House, a division of Penguin Random House LLC, New York.

DEL REY and the HOUSE colophon are registered trademarks of Penguin Random House LLC.

Published in hardcover in the United Kingdom by Egmont UK Limited.

ISBN 978-0-399-18202-0
Ebook ISBN 978-1-5247-9741-6

Printed in China on acid-free paper by C & C Offset

Written by Craig Jelley. Additional material by Stephanie Milton, Marsh Davies and Owen Jones.

Illustrations by Ryan Marsh, John Stuckey and James Bale

randomhousebooks.com

8 9 7

Design by Joe Bolder and John Stuckey

GUIDE TO:

✏ CREATIVE

CONTENTS

INTRODUCTION

Welcome to the official Guide to Creative! Almost everything you do in Minecraft involves some kind of creativity, and though true creativity is hard to teach, we're hoping this guide will inspire you to build some brilliant, beautiful things.

We've split the guide into three parts. The first section will help you plan your build. Without good preparation, even the most modest of creations can go awry. You'll learn how to use the very shape of the land to your advantage.

Next, we move on to the components you use to create your builds. Creative mode gives you access to unlimited materials but exactly which ones you use will affect the look and feel of your constructions. Hopefully, we'll stop you from getting overwhelmed by all the choices!

The third part of the guide is more concerned with the details. A few finishing touches can help your creations shine. Learn how to decorate your build and design your own personal motif, as well as how to light your designs for maximum drama.

Let your imagination run wild. Get creative!

OWEN JONES
THE MOJANG TEAM

MOJANG STUFF

Look out for these boxes throughout the book to discover super-exclusive info from the developers at Mojang.

1

PLANNING

This section introduces the simple concepts of planning your build, whether it's deciding on the best location, putting together a simple framework for your creation, or selecting textures and a colour scheme.

BEFORE YOU BEGIN

There are a few things to consider before you join the ranks of Minecraft's master builders. Follow these tips to ensure you start your creative masterpiece in the right way and set yourself up for success.

THE ADVANTAGES OF CREATIVE MODE

If you set up your world in Creative mode you'll be able to make incredible builds quickly and easily. Here's a summary of the key features that make this mode so useful to builders.

1. Hostile mobs are passive in Creative mode, so you don't have to fend them off whilst building.

2. Your hunger and health won't deplete as you work, so you don't have to worry about monitoring your food and health bars.

3. You can fly! Double press the jump button to start flight, then you're free to ascend and descend as needed, making building and decorating tall buildings much easier.

4. Rather than hunting for the rare materials that are essential to your build, you'll have access to unlimited numbers of every block, courtesy of a full creative inventory.

5. Whilst Creative mode makes it easier to construct incredible builds, you can use the tips in this book in Survival mode if you prefer. You'll just need to collect the necessary materials first.

BEGINNER'S BUILD TIPS

Attempting grand feats of architecture can be difficult at first, especially if you're used to constructing buildings to function well rather than to look nice. Following these tips will make your creative builds all the more impressive.

FIND INSPIRATION

Research the theme you want to incorporate into your build. Whether it's a busy rail station, a dwarven fortress or a medieval cathedral, you can draw from examples in books, films, TV and the internet.

BIOMES

Some biomes are easier to build in than others. If you choose a plains biome, you'll hardly need to do anything to the terrain before you can begin, but if you want to build in a roofed forest you'll need to clear a lot of vegetation first. Consider how much time you have before choosing a biome.

LOCATION, LOCATION, LOCATION

A moon base will look odd by a flowing river, as will a skyscraper peeking out the top of a jungle canopy. Spend some time scouting the right location before you begin.

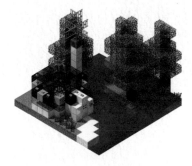

THINK OUTSIDE THE BOX

Oak wood stairs in the roof? Trapdoors for windows? The blocks in Minecraft are incredibly versatile, and have a number of unintended uses that can really enhance the look of your build.

DEPTH AND DETAIL

Full blocks are perfect for defining your build's shape, but a lot of them are lacking in detail. You can use partial blocks like slabs and stairs to create depth in walls and floors.

USING THE LAND

Where you choose to build is just as important as the build itself, so you should make sure that your ingenious idea has a setting that cleverly complements it. You can either search for the perfect location, or you can build it yourself.

BIOMES

Each biome and sub-biome in Minecraft has characteristics that lend themselves to certain types of build. Consider each biome in terms of the unique combination of these characteristics, then choose the one that is best suited to your build.

PLAINS

This flat, grassy biome has plenty of water holes and passive mobs, which makes it ideal for farmhouses, mills and industrial plants.

FOREST

An abundance of trees and plants help the forest biome lend itself to cosy cottages, treehouses and fantastical elven villages.

Swamps have large bodies of water dotted with islands, which forms a great base for a stilted pirate village or harbour.

SWAMP

The tropical blocks, items and mobs of the jungle biome lend themselves well to lost temples, botanical gardens and simple huts.

JUNGLE

The leafy taiga has snowy and mountainous variants, making it a versatile building biome.

TAIGA

ROOFED FOREST

The thick canopies of the roofed forest let in little light, which provides the perfect setting for spooky builds like decrepit temples and haunted houses.

Full of peaks and troughs, the extreme hills biome is the perfect place to build picturesque castles.

EXTREME HILLS

ICE PLAINS

Bright white snow and minimal wildlife make this biome perfect for ice palaces or isolated cabins.

Covered in dry grass and acacia trees, the wide open savanna is the perfect location for a safari park.

SAVANNA

DESERT

A bright, sandy biome, deserts are perfect for Egyptian builds like sphinxes and pyramids.

The Nether and the End both have dark, unusual terrain that is perfect for alien landscapes, lairs and hideaways, while End cities have unusual ships and buildings, creating a fantasy feel.

NETHER/END

OCEAN

Building opportunities are limited in the ocean, but underwater observatories will look spectacular.

MUSHROOM ISLAND

The bizarre vegetation of this biome lends itself to quirky, fantasy-themed builds like fairy cottages.

MESA

Wild west saloons and sheriff offices look great against the red sand and canyons of the mesa.

NATURAL FEATURES

From simple rivers to more complex structures like villages, the Minecraft landscape is a source of many natural features. These features can be integrated into your builds, either as they are or with a little customisation. Work with the landscape to create something truly impressive.

1 Rivers and lakes flow through most biomes and can add interest to your builds. This simple water mill looks great next to a river flowing into a village.

2 Home to friendly villagers, the village is a hub of trading. You could add to the village, or even modernise the simple buildings that feature throughout.

3 Abandoned mineshafts are another feature found underground, rich in ores and filled with streams of lava. Their resources make them the perfect front for an industrial build.

4 Waterfalls are one of the more impressive natural features. Building anything atop or across the cascade will look amazing.

5 Desert and jungle temples are elaborate structures found in the desert and jungle biomes respectively. They make the perfect centrepiece for historical or ancient builds.

6 Lava can add an air of danger or evil to your builds. Funnelling a lava river around your castle will make invaders think twice about approaching.

Strongholds, home to end portals and libraries, are also found underground. You can build a base on top of one and use it as a secret lair.

If none of these features or structures have a place in your plan, then you can always create your own terrain for your builds. If you have enough time you could make anything from a giant quartz moon crater to a snowy stone city, or a colourful candyland.

AESTHETICS

The blocks you choose for your structure will define the look and character of your build. From the colour schemes and block textures of your build's base to the unique finishing touches, every detail is important.

COLOURS

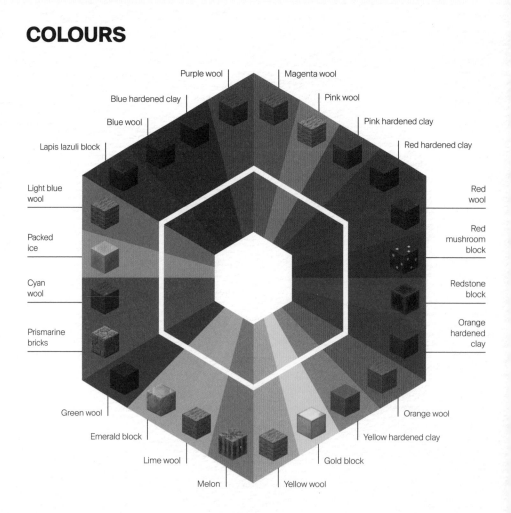

Purple wool

Magenta wool

Blue hardened clay

Pink wool

Blue wool

Pink hardened clay

Lapis lazuli block

Red hardened clay

Light blue wool

Red wool

Packed ice

Red mushroom block

Cyan wool

Redstone block

Prismarine bricks

Orange hardened clay

Green wool

Orange wool

Emerald block

Yellow hardened clay

Lime wool

Gold block

Melon

Yellow wool

COLOUR WHEEL
The colour wheel is a handy tool for choosing a colour scheme for your build. The wheel covers the whole spectrum of colours, which change in subtle gradients. The colours interact in different ways with the colours around them to create a variety of colour schemes, which can be used to accent a building's exterior, or decorate its interior rooms.

ANALOGUE COLOURS

An analogue colour scheme is the simplest. This requires that you choose two or three blocks adjacent to each other on the colour wheel. For instance, you could make a colour scheme using gold, yellow wool and yellow hardened clay blocks.

COMPLEMENTARY COLOURS

Complementary colour schemes are made by choosing blocks directly opposite on the colour wheel. These colours will contrast dramatically, but still look good together.

TRIADIC COLOURS

A triadic colour scheme is slightly more complicated. Choose three blocks equally spaced out on the colour wheel to create this scheme and give your build greater variety and interest.

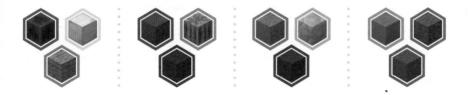

MONOCHROMATIC SCALE

The monochromatic scale uses a spectrum of shades between black and white. Black is classed as the absence of colour, while white is the combination of all colours. Black and white contrast with each other, but can also be used to balance a build that involves lots of colourful blocks.

ADDING DEPTH

One way to fine-tune the outside of your build is to add depth. This is easy to do and results in more points of interest rather than endless flat surfaces. The best blocks for creating depth are partial blocks like stairs and slabs since they are a different shape and size to regular blocks.

Stairs and slabs can also be used to replace regular blocks in walls.

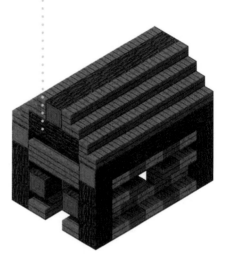

Stairs and slabs can be placed on the side of flat walls to create decorative features.

Another way to create depth is to make your walls two or more blocks thick. This allows you to create patterns by removing some of the outer blocks.

You could also combine these ideas and use partial blocks in a double thickness wall.

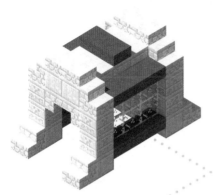

Glass panes sit in the middle of wall blocks, unlike glass blocks, which sit flush with the outer edge.

Glass can also be set into a small extension to make bay-style windows.

You can use partial blocks to create window sills and awnings over windows.

Did you add any overhangs to your build? Use upside-down stairs to create support brackets for them.

Doors, slabs and stairs can be used to make doorsteps and decorative areas above door frames.

AESTHETIC THEMES

Some blocks inherently lend themselves to certain themes. This can be down to the colour of the block, or the texture of it. By combining carefully-selected base blocks you can create endless themed builds. Take inspiration from these examples and create some of your own ideas.

Steampunk style features steam-powered industrial details like wheels, cogs and clocks.

STEAMPUNK

INDUSTRIAL

For an industrial vibe, use a generous amount of manufactured blocks like iron and glass.

Recreate Minecraft's hellish underworld with the Nether's native blocks and plenty of lava.

INFERNAL

If a spooky dwelling is more your thing, pair dark wood blocks with orange hues and jack o'lanterns.

SPOOKY

HISTORICAL

Sand and sandstone help to give your build an ancient and historical feel.

A fantasy build should be unusual and look like it comes from a different world entirely.

FANTASY

Choose clean, white blocks and subtle chiselled details for a classical build.

Simple wood and stone blocks lend themselves to a rustic-themed build like this woodland cottage.

RUSTIC

CLASSICAL

BLOCK HACKS

There are hundreds of blocks available for use in your constructions. Many of them have a clear purpose, but, with a little imagination, you can also use them in unexpected ways. Check out these clever block hacks for the exterior of your builds.

1 Stairs are perfect for building roofs as they look like staggered tiling. They're available in a variety of woods and stones and can be worked into many different build styles.

2 Cobblestone walls make excellent boundary markers for the perimeter of a build, but they can also be used as supports for raised structures like lookouts and balconies.

3 Usually used to keep mobs and animals at bay, fences can also save you from falls by lining stairs, balconies and roofs.

MOJANG STUFF

Interior designers might take advantage of one of Jeb's favourite block hacks. Take a fence pole then place a leaf block on top for a quaint indoor shrub.

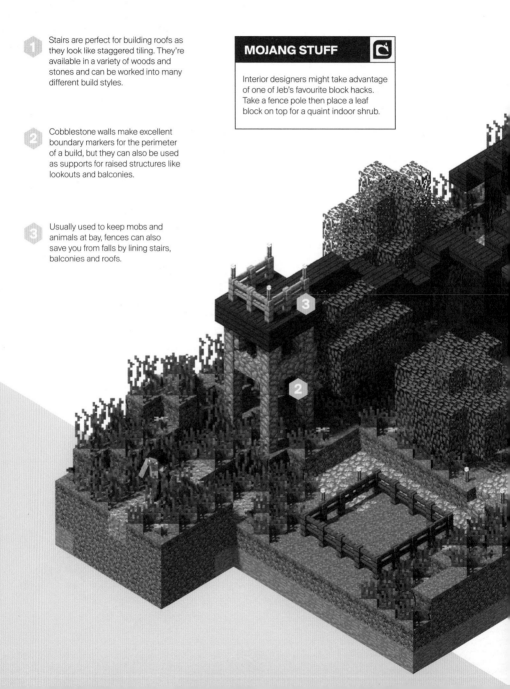

Cobwebs seem like a relatively useless item, but can be used around chimneys and fires to give the impression of billowing smoke.

Trapdoors can be used to create rustic windows. An advantage of using these over glass panes is that they can be opened and closed.

Place a torch on an outside wall, then an item frame over the top of it, and finally a stone slab to give the effect of a medieval wall-mounted torch.

STRUCTURE

It's important to get the structure of your constructions right so that the rest of the build will go according to plan. Once you have an idea, the next step is to plan it out and begin to lay the foundations.

SHAPES

The shape of your build affects everything from the foundations to the roof. For many builders simplicity is key, but more complicated shapes, which are harder to get right, can make for a truly impressive build. Take inspiration from these simple shapes to get you started.

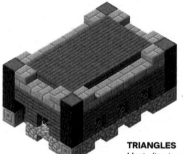

QUADRILATERALS
Squares and rectangles are the easiest shapes to make. Use them as a base for simple, four-sided rooms, and to create flat walls. They are perfect for simple builds.

TRIANGLES
Most often incorporated into roofs, triangles can also be used as a base if you're happy to have diagonal walls. Be aware that this could make it awkward to decorate inside, or to join to other builds.

CIRCLES
Flying in the face of Minecraft's blocky nature, circles are often integrated into more impressive builds. The tricky part is knowing how to successfully make curves – consult the outlines below for guidance.

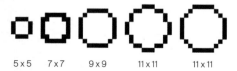

5 x 5   7 x 7   9 x 9   11 x 11   11 x 11

PYRAMIDS

The pyramid is an iconic shape from the landmarks of Egypt. Begin with a large square base, then build upwards.

SPHERES

Small spheres can be incorporated into builds to add detail, but, for a real challenge, try building a spherical base. Look at the instructions below to find out how to build one. You can even make one by adding circles to the sides of a cube.

TRIANGULAR PRISMS

Built in a similar way to pyramids, triangular prisms are most commonly associated with attics and tents.

11 x 11

11 x 11

9 x 9

7 x 7

5 x 5

1 Using the yellow outlines here as a guide, build five circles of increasing size.

2 Build another circle exactly the same size as the largest of the five circles.

3 Now build four more circles of decreasing size in the opposite direction. This will give you a perfect Minecraft sphere.

BUILD FRAMEWORK

Once you've chosen a shape for your build you can create the framework. Starting from the ground and working upwards, follow these steps to create the outer framework and add internal levels. We've chosen a simple rectangular build to outline the process.

1 Use cobblestone to mark the base of your build on the ground, then place your doors in the desired location.

2 Build upwards from each corner of your base until you have the frame for your ground floor. Now fill in your ground floor and first floor, leaving space in the first floor for a staircase.

3 If you want your first floor to be the same size as the ground floor, simply build upwards in each corner of your first floor. Alternatively you could expand this floor, creating an overhang outside.

BUILDING BLOCKS

7 Add some interest to the land around your build. This can include torches for lighting, pathways, flower beds and trees.

6 Aim for the bottom half of each dirt block when placing stair blocks, otherwise they'll be upside-down. Add extra blocks at the edges to create overhangs.

5 Add glass to your window spaces, then create a base for your roof using dirt blocks. You can destroy these once the roof is in place.

4 Decide where you will place windows, then fill in your walls leaving the desired amount of space for them.

ARCHITECTURAL STRUCTURES

Once the basic framework of your build is complete, you can adapt it with a variety of decorative and functional structures. Take inspiration from real-life architecture and add some finishing touches and iconic features to finish off the exterior of your build.

ARCH

A decorative adornment for buildings, arches are often used to frame doors and windows. They can also be a supporting structure, forming a walkway underneath part of a building.

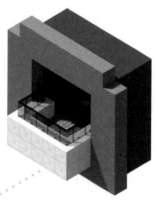

BALCONY

A small outdoor platform that extends out from the wall, a balcony is accessed via a door from the building, and enclosed by walls or rails.

BAY WINDOW

A bay window is a type of window that extends out of the wall, forming a bay within a room and providing extra space, with a view of the area outside.

COLONNADE

A series of columns is called a colonnade. These can be added to porches, ornamental features, or set into walls to create depth.

CHIMNEY

Chimneys funnel fumes and smoke out of houses. Much bigger examples can be seen on industrial buildings.

CUPOLA

Sometimes used for ventilation, but mostly ornamental, cupolas are square or circular structures that crown buildings. They're often seen on temples, cathedrals and even farmhouses.

CORNICE

This is the decorative flourish on a structural corner. Just add two upside-down stairs to the top corner of a build to create a cornice.

FLYING BUTTRESS

An arched structure used in huge builds, flying buttresses provide additional support to walls and roofs and make for striking decorative features. Flying buttresses are often seen on the exterior of cathedrals.

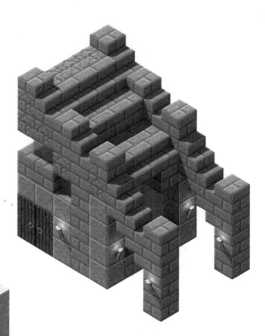

GABLE

A gable is the triangular area of wall between two roof pitches. Adding windows to a gable will provide light for an attic space in the roof.

FRIEZE

This is a row of decorative bricks or blocks that breaks up a plain wall. They are often seen in ancient and classical structures.

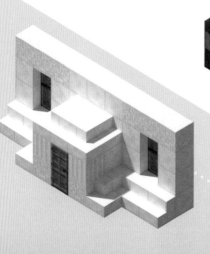

PORTICO

Also known as a simple porch, this is a permanent structure attached to a building, with a roof and solid supports.

ROOF TERRACE
A roof terrace is an open space on top of a building, surrounded by low parapet walls. They are often used as green spaces in otherwise grey cities.

SPIRE
A spire is a tapered addition to the top of a building. Traditionally they were a celestial gesture, reaching towards the sky on churches and cathedrals. In modern architecture, spires are often seen at the top of city skyscrapers. Aircraft warning lights are often placed at the very top of skyscraper spires to ensure low-flying aircraft don't hit them.

LINKING BUILDS

Now you've got the exterior of your build completed, you can consider how it interacts with other buildings. Having lots of separate builds will leave a lot of negative space (unused space) between them. Here are some ways to turn that negative space into something cool, and combine your buildings in effective and attractive ways.

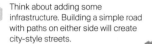 Think about adding some infrastructure. Building a simple road with paths on either side will create city-style streets.

Find ways to integrate your buildings into the space – add staircases from raised doors to street level, for example.

3 If your building's ground floor is smaller than the first floor, you'll have empty space underneath. Turn this into a public space or a car park.

4 Use the space between your buildings to create other features. In this instance, the park is connected to the streets and surrounding areas of the building by a number of pathways.

5 Create fire escapes for multi-storey buildings from iron bars, slabs and ladders.

6 You can avoid negative space entirely by positioning your builds directly next to each other, like terraced houses.

7 Why stay above ground? Tunnel underneath the surface to create subways, or make entrances to cellars beneath the buildings.

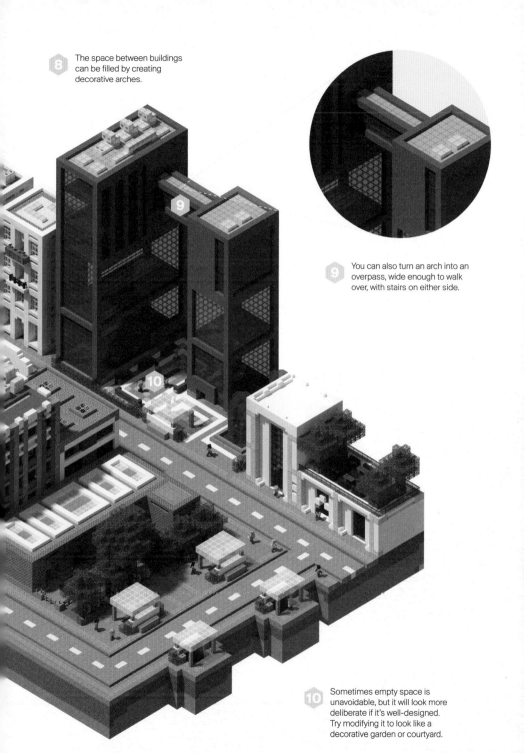

8 The space between buildings can be filled by creating decorative arches.

9 You can also turn an arch into an overpass, wide enough to walk over, with stairs on either side.

10 Sometimes empty space is unavoidable, but it will look more deliberate if it's well-designed. Try modifying it to look like a decorative garden or courtyard.

DECORATION

Now you've created the frame of your builds you can add character with some carefully selected decoration. This section contains ideas for decorating floors and walls, clever designs for interior decor, and inspiration to help you make the most of external spaces.

FUNCTIONAL DECOR

There are dozens of blocks in Minecraft that perform useful functions, but they can also double as decorative items too. Let's take a look at these versatile blocks in more detail and learn how to weave them into your creation.

LIGHTING

Light can come from various sources in the Minecraft world: naturally from the sun and moon, from light-emitting blocks, or when activated as a part of a redstone circuit. Some light sources may be quite unexpected.

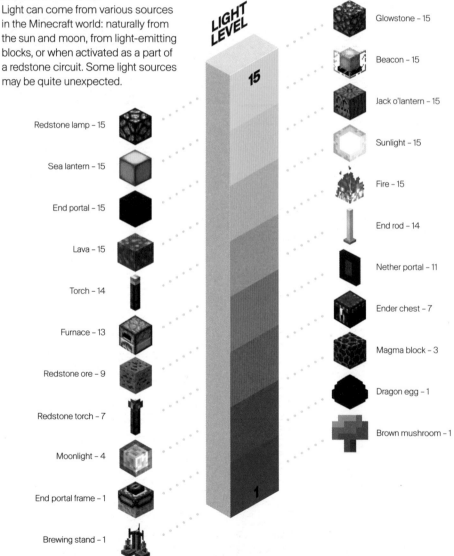

LIGHT LEVEL

15

1

Redstone lamp – 15

Sea lantern – 15

End portal – 15

Lava – 15

Torch – 14

Furnace – 13

Redstone ore – 9

Redstone torch – 7

Moonlight – 4

End portal frame – 1

Brewing stand – 1

Glowstone – 15

Beacon – 15

Jack o'lantern – 15

Sunlight – 15

Fire – 15

End rod – 14

Nether portal – 11

Ender chest – 7

Magma block – 3

Dragon egg – 1

Brown mushroom – 1

LIGHT FIXTURES AND FEATURES

Now you know which blocks emit light, here are some clever ideas to harness them and make unique features to illuminate your constructions.

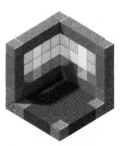

COLOURFUL WINDOW
Take advantage of natural light by creating stained glass windows. See pages 42-43 for more info.

CHANDELIER
Simple End rods can be turned into fancy chandeliers by attaching them to fences.

COSY FIREPLACE
Make a fireplace by combining netherrack with cobblestone and iron bars.

FRAMED LIGHTING
Add torches and slabs to item frames to create unusual interior lighting.

BEACON
Exterior beacons can be created from netherrack, brick stairs and fences.

INSET LIGHTING
Light-emitting blocks can feature in walls and floors for unobtrusive lighting.

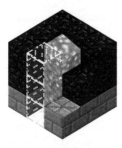

LAVA LAMPLIGHT
Utilise lava as a light feature by pouring it into wall cavities covered with glass.

LAMP POST
Fire-topped netherrack can be housed in wooden trapdoors to let light out.

ARTY LIGHT INSTALLATION
Combine stained glass and glowstone to create colourful and arty light features.

UTILITY BLOCKS

Minecraft has many utility blocks - blocks that perform valuable functions. Many of these fit obviously into certain styles of builds. The following themed builds showcase some of these blocks and how they might be used for decoration.

RUSTIC WORKSHOP

The raw, unpolished finish of the furnace and anvil blends well with the basic wooden textures of the crafting table and chest, in addition to the room itself, which is constructed from wood and stone.

CHEST
Useful for item and tool storage, the chest is a necessity.

CRAFTING TABLE
Crafted itself from wood, it fits in seamlessly with the rustic workshop.

ANVIL
The raw, black finish of the anvil complements this simple build.

FURNACE
The rough stone of the furnace is well suited to the workshop aesthetic.

MYSTIC LAIR

Bookshelves, ender chests and enchantment tables lend their mystical aesthetic to builds like clandestine hideouts or underground lairs.

BOOKSHELVES
Full of magical tomes written in an indecipherable language, bookshelves add colour and mystery.

CAULDRON
Usually found in witch huts, cauldrons are an obvious choice for any mystical build.

ENDER CHEST
A form of storage forged in the ethereal End, the ender chest is at home in a mystical lair.

BREWING STAND
A brewing stand is ideal decoration for a magical room since it produces all manner of powerful potions.

MODERN DEN

More modern blocks such as the jukebox, armour stands and beds fit perfectly in a minimalist, modern den.

JUKEBOX
A fun Minecraft device, no modern build would be complete without a jukebox to play music.

SHULKER BOX
Shulker boxes can be altered with dye, making them easy to fit into any modern room.

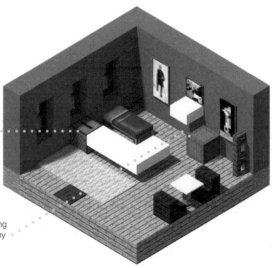

AESTHETIC DECOR

As well as incorporating useful function blocks, you'll want to create something bespoke for your build so that it stands out. This section covers decorative features that you can combine to make your builds unique.

WINDOWS

Windows can make great decorative features on your build. Here are just a few ways to make eye-catching window features from a variety of glass blocks.

SHAPED WINDOWS
Windows don't have to be rectangular - glass can be placed in shapes within the wall. Use the guide to shapes on page 24 if you need to refresh your memory.

ORNATE WINDOWS
Glass can be combined into intricate patterns or elaborate designs, like those found on castles, temples and other extravagant buildings.

BLOCKS VERSUS PANES
Consider whether to use blocks or panes. Blocks fill the whole block space, while panes are inset and sit in the middle of a block space.

GLASS BUILDINGS
For a striking, modern
effect, why not use glass
for the majority of the
build's exterior? This will
make rooms brighter
and feel more spacious.

PICTORIAL WINDOWS
Stained glass can even
be used to make colourful
pictures, from simple flowers
to more complicated pixel art.

COLOURED GLASS
You can use stained glass
panes and blocks to add some
colour to plain walls, or to
complement a colour scheme.

WALLS AND FLOORS

There are many ways to customise the walls and floors of your builds and add a little artistic flair. Let's take a look at some of the blocks you can use and how they are best suited to different rooms and areas.

AREA RUGS
These can be made from carpet and placed over wooden floorboards. They work well in open spaces like living rooms.

CARPET
Wall-to-wall carpet is ideal for cosy areas like bedrooms and can help bring a bold splash of colour to your rooms.

PARTIAL WALLS
Glass, fence blocks and iron bars can be used to create physical barriers between rooms without visibly closing areas off completely. This can give your builds a more open-plan feel.

CHECKERBOARD TILES

A classic checkerboard tile effect will look good anywhere but is particularly well-suited to kitchens and hallways.

TIP

Make your walls two-blocks thick – one wall will be your exterior design, while the other will be the interior pattern that you choose.

FEATURE WALLS

The blocks you construct your buildings with will dictate what your interior walls are made of and will often be exposed brick or stone. You can add another layer on top of your walls to create a colourful feature wall.

MOSAIC TILES

Hardened clay can be used to create mosaic tiles suited to hallways, foyers and formal areas.

PAINTINGS AND ITEM FRAMES

Some functional blocks are decorative by design. Paintings provide an artistic splash of colour for your interiors – the smallest covers just a single block, while the largest will span a 4 x 4-block area. Item frames allow you to display meaningful items on your walls.

PAINTINGS
There are 26 available paintings. The smallest are 1 x 1 block, and the largest are an impressive 4 x 4 blocks. Keep placing and destroying them until you get the one you want.

TIP

Paintings can be used to conceal entrances to secret rooms if they are placed over a 1 x 2 block gap.

PAINTING PLACEMENT
Painting placement is random and also depends on the available space. You won't know which painting you're getting until you place it on a vertical surface, when a random painting will appear.

ITEM FRAMES
Item frames can be placed on plinths or walls to display everything from your favourite armour and weapons to maps or spawn eggs. They make great features for museums or galleries.

TIP

Once they've been placed in a frame, items can be rotated. Try rotating an arrow to make a stylish signpost.

BANNERS

Minecraft's most customisable block is the banner. Using dyes and a few other items, you can create patterned banners to use as wallpapers, signs and decorations for any build. Here are the basic patterns. You can use whichever dye you like.

HALVES

Bold blocks of colour form a good base for an asymmetric banner.

STRIPES

Swashes of colour will cut through a more dominant base.

   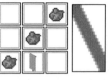 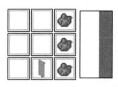 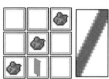

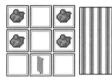

BORDERS AND BACKGROUNDS

Simple patterns can frame a creation, or form a detailed background.

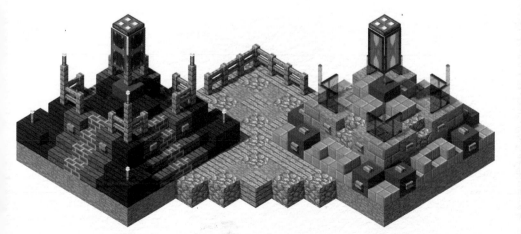

GRADIENTS

Subtle, gradual changes in colour cover the whole banner.

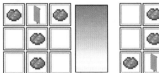 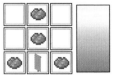

SHAPES

Small shapes can be combined and scattered across simple backgrounds.

ICONS

Interesting pictures are best placed as a top layer on a banner.

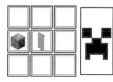  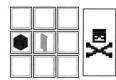  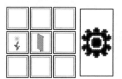  

LAYERING

You can place up to 6 different patterns on a banner to create unique combinations like the ones here. If you make a mistake then you can remove the last pattern you placed by using the banner on a cauldron to wash it off.

DISPLAYING

As well as using banners to decorate the interior of builds, you can create structures specifically designed to show them off. They can be placed on full or partial blocks and displayed on your build's exterior.

FURNITURE HACKS

The interior of your building is taking shape nicely, but it is still a little bare. Several blocks can be used in imaginative ways to create pieces of furniture. Let's take a look at some of the most common block hacks and what can be created with them.

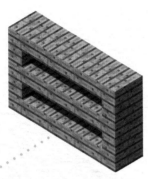

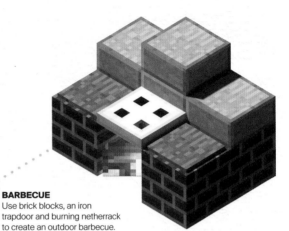

SHELVES
Stair and slab blocks can be used to create shelves for your walls.

BARBECUE
Use brick blocks, an iron trapdoor and burning netherrack to create an outdoor barbecue.

MIRROR
Place packed ice into walls to create mirrors above your sinks.

SINK
Keep yourself clean with a sink made from hoppers, quartz slabs and a lever.

BATH
Create a luxurious bathtub with quartz stairs, dark prismarine blocks and levers for taps.

TOILET
Create a toilet – a bathroom essential – with a quartz slab, quartz block, pressure plate and button.

COMPUTER
Place a painting on the back of a stair block and a pressure plate in front to make a computer.

GRAND PIANO
For musical entertainment, create a grand piano from wood plank slabs, fences and rails.

GRANDFATHER CLOCK
With this timepiece, made from trapdoors and a clock inside an item frame, you'll never be late.

CHAIR
Living spaces need lots of seating, so create these armchairs out of stairs and signs.

SOFA
Turn stair blocks into long settees and create arms at each end using sign blocks.

FIREPLACE
Make your build cosy in the cold with a fireplace. Light netherrack inside a cobblestone chimney.

DJ DECKS
Mix pressure plates, note blocks and a lever-activated redstone lamp to create a sound system.

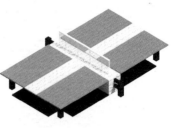

SMALL TABLE
For a single-space table, place a redstone torch under pistons that are facing upwards.

FAMILY TABLE
Place carpet on top of torches or fences to create longer tables to seat more guests.

PING-PONG TABLE
Create your own ping-pong table with carpet, glass panes, wool and fences.

TELEVISION
Cover a 4 x 2 set of black wool with a painting to create a television, then add jukeboxes either side as speakers.

POOL TABLE
Surround a 3 x 2 block of green wool with trapdoors to create a pool table. Snowballs and slimeballs are nice finishing touches.

BUNK BEDS
Place beds on top of slabs jutting out of the wall to create bunk beds, perfect for dorms and bedrooms.

WINDOW BOXES
You can make attractive window boxes using dirt placed against a wall, trapdoors and flowers.

FRIDGE
For cleverly storing food, use an iron block, iron door, dispenser and button to make a fridge.

STOVE
What kitchen is complete without an oven? Place a trapdoor on top of a furnace to make a hob.

FOUR-POSTER BED
If a regular bed isn't fancy enough, use wood blocks, fences and trapdoors to create a four-poster.

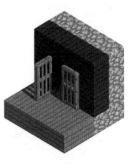

WARDROBE
Use a small alcove to create a wardrobe – add armour stands and place wooden doors at the front.

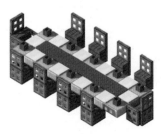

FORMAL DINING TABLE
Make a formal dining table with gold weighted pressure plates, red carpet and flower pots.

OUTDOOR SPACES

The area around your build deserves as much attention as the build itself. The next few pages showcase some inspired ways to make the most of your outdoor space so that your build flows seamlessly into its environment.

1 WATER FEATURES
Ponds and streams can be added to outdoor spaces as focal points. Dig an area then use water buckets to fill it. You can build bridges over your water features, or place lily pads on the surface to create a walkable path. Fountains can provide centrepieces too.

2 FENCES
These wooden blocks come in six styles and can be used to mark the outer edge of a build and protect items within. Stacking them and combining with gates makes for an interesting entrance too.

3 FLOWERS
Your outdoor area could benefit from the addition of flowers. Available in all the colours of the rainbow, they can be used for beautiful patterns or as small highlights in otherwise green areas.

TREES

There are saplings for every type of tree in the game. You can pick your favourite and plant the corresponding saplings in your outdoor space to create a lush border to your outdoor space, or even your own forest.

TREE POSITIONING

Each type of tree requires a different number of free blocks above where it is planted. Consult the chart to see how many spaces are required for your desired trees.

For dark oak, giant spruce and giant jungle trees, you'll need to plant four saplings in a 2 x 2 square.

Oak | Birch | Jungle | Spruce | Acacia | Dark Oak | Giant Jungle | Giant Spruce

HEDGES

Like fences, leaves can be used to create partitions and borders around your build. However, they offer more freedom as they're a traditional block and can be formed into shapes more easily.

DESIGN YOUR OWN TREES

It can take a while for saplings to grow, but you can skip the wait and design your own trees. Wood and leaves obviously work well and can be combined in new ways, but you can also experiment with more unusual designs and different blocks.

SPHERICAL TREE
Put your sphere-making skills to good use and create neat, spherical trees for a stylish garden.

SPOOKY TREE
Create a spooky, bare tree from wood blocks and hanging jack o'lanterns. The more crooked you can make the trunk and branches, the better.

CANDYFLOSS TREE
For a fantasy build, use colourful blocks instead of wood and leaves. This candyfloss tree is perfect for a fantasy candyland.

BONSAI TREE
After something a little more ornamental? Create a pretty, full-size bonsai tree with carefully crafted branches and foliage.

ADDITIONAL STRUCTURES

Now that you have the basics of your outdoor area in place you can add some more complex structures to help personalise the space and bring it to life.

MEETING POINTS

Outdoor areas are often dotted with meeting points and social venues. You can make your outdoor area into a public space with additions like bandstands and open terraces.

BRIDGES

Bridges are the easiest way to cross the rivers, lakes and streams of your outdoor space. These can range from simple wooden footpaths to elaborately sculpted crossings.

ARCHES

Basic pathways can be upgraded with the addition of some decorative arches. These can serve as gateways to different areas, or just brighten up an otherwise dull walk.

COMMUNAL SPACE

Outdoor spaces are the perfect location for communities to come together and create. Whether it's a public garden or a communal greenhouse, locals can add to and benefit from these additions.

MAZES

Leafy hedges can be used to fill and transform space into intricate mazes. Mark out the route to the end point on the floor first, then create walkways and dead ends all around it.

3

BUILDING

Now you've learnt how to plan and decorate builds, this section shows you how to incorporate your new-found skills into cohesive structures. You'll see builds that cross different themes, styles, functions and locations to inspire more of your own ideas.

REMOTE OUTPOST

This secluded outpost incorporates a natural theme combining wood, diorite and cobblestone. Slabs and stairs add depth to the exterior features, while the simple interior is split between two floors across two complementary structures.

TIP

Create a billowing flag by using wool blocks. Place them at different depths to make it look like it's blowing in the wind.

RUSTIC THEME

COMPLEMENTARY

SCHEMATICS

These plans show the sentry outpost from various perspectives. The turret base begins as part of the main building, sharing the ground floor, and cuts through the roof. There is no first floor within the turret, but there is an accessible rooftop.

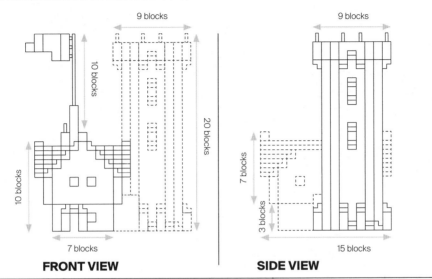

FRONT VIEW

9 blocks

10 blocks

20 blocks

10 blocks

7 blocks

SIDE VIEW

9 blocks

7 blocks

3 blocks

15 blocks

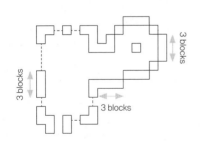

GROUND FLOOR

3 blocks

3 blocks

3 blocks

FIRST FLOOR

7 blocks

3 blocks

11 blocks

EXTREME HILLS

IDEAL LANDSCAPE

A remote sentry outpost is most useful when positioned at a good vantage point, but in an obscured spot. The best location to place this build is on a high mountain, surrounded by tall trees. Clear a flat piece of land in an extreme hills biome before laying the foundations.

REMOTE OUTPOST EXTERIOR

1 Create a colourful flag. This could be a pattern you like, or colours that signify your alliance with a group.

2 The exterior lighting is a makeshift beacon, used for signalling other outposts or villages in the area. The trapdoor encasement can be opened and closed to modify visibility.

3 The land space of the outpost is enclosed in a simple cobblestone wall and filled with flowers, small trees and lighting.

The highest point of the outpost – the lookout on top of the turret – allows visibility of the surrounding area.

Borrowed from medieval architecture, the turret provides additional defence against any potential attackers. It has no exterior entrances and is made from strong cobblestone.

Wells provide a source of fresh water to the outpost, which might otherwise be difficult to find on high ground.

REMOTE OUTPOST INTERIOR

1 The interior comforts are basic – a solitary chair and table, a single bed and chests for storage of foraged resources.

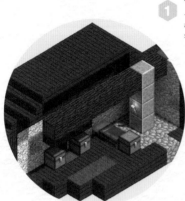

2 The interior lighting consists of a few torches placed on the walls. This makes the outpost less visible at night and requires fewer resources.

3 The open stone fireplace is the only source of warmth in the outpost, placed directly underneath the chimney so smoke can escape.

Inside the turret there is a spiral staircase and ladder leading to a trapdoor, which separates the interior from the rooftop lookout.

The remote outpost has many workstations, used to craft resources into useful tools, food and weapons to help survive the wilderness.

LIGHTING SYSTEM

You'll need a lighting system to illuminate your creations. Lights can be activated manually by a switch, or set to come on automatically. This example shows how to incorporate a lighting system into a simple house with two rooms.

1 Build a second wall around your house, with a single-block gap in between the two. This will contain all of your redstone.

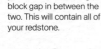

2 Add a lever to one of your interior wall blocks. This will control the lighting system for the entire building so place it somewhere convenient.

3 Start your vertical transmission circuit behind the lever. There's a redstone torch behind the wall block with alternating blocks and redstone torches above it.

Now your lighting system is finished, you can complete the rest of the construction. Make sure to cover up the wiring – here we've hidden it in the attic space.

Position your redstone lamps, then add redstone across beams through the centre of the room, and link back to the vertical transmission with redstone dust.

When the vertical transmission has reached the ceiling, create a block grid above the gap in between your walls.

LIGHTING SYSTEM VARIATIONS

Larger builds may benefit from having several independent circuits so the lighting can be customised for each room or area. Let's take a look at some internal lighting ideas as well as options for the exterior of your builds.

1 FLOOR LIGHTING
Floor lighting is a stylish alternative to wall or ceiling lights and works well in bathrooms and kitchens. It's powered by redstone hidden underneath the floor blocks.

2 SECURITY LIGHTING
In external areas your lighting can be connected to a tripwire or to pressure plates. The system will be activated when mobs or enemy players trespass on your land, providing effective security lighting.

AUTOMATIC LIGHTING

For ultimate convenience, try an automatic lighting system. It's controlled by daylight sensors placed on the roof so there's no need for levers or buttons – it'll come on as soon as the sun sets.

TIP

For permanent under-floor lighting, replace the redstone circuitry with a simple redstone torch under each lamp.

EXOTIC VILLA

An archetype of Mediterranean architecture, this stylish villa incorporates classical features in a luxury residence. The minimalist colour scheme is complemented with splashes of colour inside, and contrasted by an extravagant outdoor space.

CLASSICAL THEME

MONOCHROMATIC ANALOGUE

SCHEMATICS

The simplistic cuboid shape of the villa is embellished with various features that add depth and interest to the build, from colonnades and arches to cornices and gables. The interior has an intermediate level, called a mezzanine, between the ground and first floors.

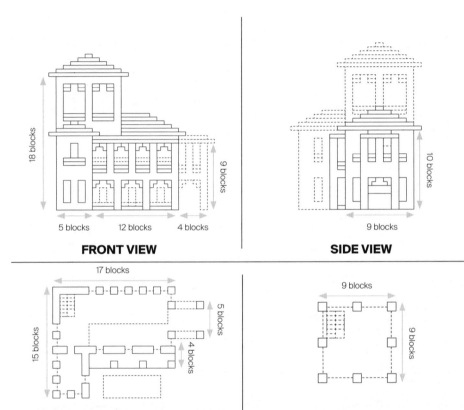

FRONT VIEW

18 blocks

9 blocks

5 blocks 12 blocks 4 blocks

SIDE VIEW

10 blocks

9 blocks

GROUND FLOOR

17 blocks

15 blocks

5 blocks

4 blocks

FIRST FLOOR

9 blocks

9 blocks

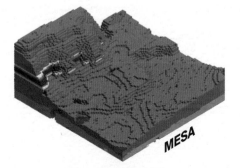

MESA

IDEAL LANDSCAPE

The Mediterranean is usually very hot, so the scorched red sand and hardened clay of the mesa biome provides the perfect staging for the villa. It's equally suitable at the top of one of the mesa's many peaks or situated in a wide open plateau.

EXOTIC VILLA EXTERIOR

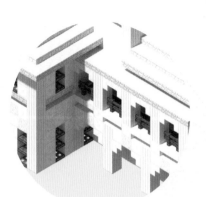

1 The build incorporates a monochromatic analogue scale, using just a few shades of white blocks. Any use of colour really stands out, including furniture and decorative blocks.

2 The colonnades that surround the villa help support the roof, while the chiselled quartz columns themselves are a similar style to those found in classical architecture.

3 The outdoor area features many leafy trees. There's a long swimming pool and a barbecue to entertain guests, and plenty of seating for everyone.

Windows are often shuttered in Mediterranean buildings. This lets air into the room, but keeps out the blazing sunlight.

5 Balconies have been added to many of the rooms on the first floor. They jut out from the main building and are surrounded by stone balustrades.

6 The doorways are framed by arches, mirrored at the front and back of the villa, with a semicircular transom (strengthening crossbar) in between the doors and outer arch.

EXOTIC VILLA INTERIOR

1 The villa has an automatic lighting system, as shown in the previous build. The inverted daylight sensor triggers the lighting to illuminate the villa as soon as the sun goes down.

2 The luxurious bedroom has a grand four-poster bed, storage chests and a walk-in wardrobe to store armour and other items.

3 The bathroom contains all the necessary features – a wet room with a shower, a large bath, toilet and sink.

4 The spacious living area features a mezzanine, a level between the ground floor and first floor, to maximize the vertical space.

5 A grand piano dominates the living area, along with a large entertainment system, myriad seating areas and an open fireplace for when winter finally sets in.

VERTICAL TRANSPORT SYSTEM

The distance between sea level and bedrock is 62 blocks, and it can be difficult to transport goods from the bottom of the world to the top, and vice versa. This clever vertical transport system will automate the process for you.

1 The entire transport system will be built within a 5 x 5 vertical shaft. Create a 5 x 5 base at your chosen underground location.

2 In this example the system runs from the top of the world to the bottom. This step shows the bottom of the system. You'll need to place a hopper behind a chest and a comparator two blocks away to monitor the chest's contents.

3 Now add your redstone circuitry. Add the extra clay blocks first, then the redstone and the redstone torch as shown.

4 Place a powered rail on top of the hopper. When a minecart with a full chest reaches the hopper it will release its contents. Once the chest is empty the cart is sent back up the track.

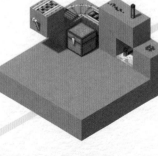

Now build the rest of your track until it reaches the surface. You'll need to use a staircase design with sharp turns so it is compact enough to fit within the 5 x 5 space.

Add a block in front of and to the left of the comparator. Once the cart reaches the top, it won't move again until the comparator detects it has been filled.

At the top of the system, add a hopper above a final powered rail, and another beside it with a chest on top. Add a comparator on a raised block directly behind the powered rail, and redstone dust on the two blocks behind it.

TRANSPORT SYSTEM ALTERNATIVES

There are many ways to customise and expand on a vertical transport system. Take inspiration from the alternatives on this page.

 MANUAL HOPPER SYSTEM
If you will be mining in multiple locations you can create a simple hopper system that doesn't require redstone circuitry.

TERMINAL
One way to disguise your redstone circuitry is to build a terminal at ground level.

UNDERGROUND SYSTEM
You can build an entire underground system to link different mining areas. If you want to switch your track at junctions simply place a lever or button as shown.

OCEAN OBSERVATORY

This ocean observatory is a glass megastructure based around a modified dome, with an entrance above sea level. Built from sturdy iron with glass for easy observation, its underwater location is something of an industrial accomplishment.

SCHEMATICS

The majority of the observatory is situated underwater, but the central shaft ascends to the surface, where it is linked to a departure platform for boats. The space within the dome is small, so there are no individual rooms, rather everything is situated in an open-plan environment.

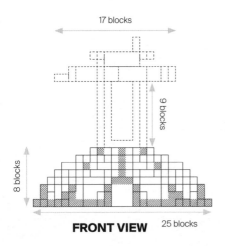

FRONT VIEW

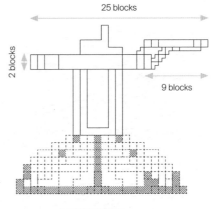

SIDE VIEW

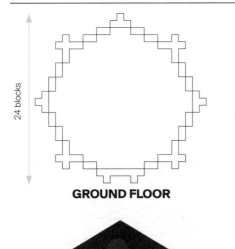

GROUND FLOOR

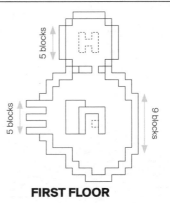

FIRST FLOOR

IDEAL LANDSCAPE

The isolated depths of the ocean biome offer a prime location for the ocean observatory, although lake and river beds would also suffice. It's best to situate the observatory towards the edge of the ocean biome so that land and resources are also accessible.

OCEAN OBSERVATORY EXTERIOR

1 The central shaft is wide enough to incorporate a transport system. The redstone circuitry can be housed within the dome, or in an annex attached to the dome.

2 The dome is the top half of a sphere, made from layered concentric circles, with a single cylindrical entrance through the top.

3 Glass blocks have been used rather than glass panes, as they are easier to construct shapes with.

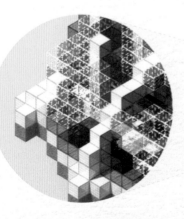

4 The port at the top of the shaft aids travel between the observatory and land. It has lots of space for loading and unloading goods.

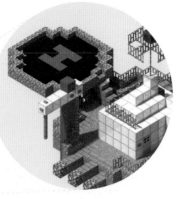

5 A huge structure such as this would require support, particularly deep underwater where pressure is greater. Flying buttresses added to the outside and columns inside provide this support.

6 The observatory is anchored underwater by iron foundations, which encircle the base of the dome, both inside and out.

OCEAN OBSERVATORY INTERIOR

1 Space is at a premium for the inhabitants of the observatory, so bunks are stacked to provide sufficient sleeping quarters.

2 Everyone working in the observatory has access to a research station, consisting of a desktop computer and testing area.

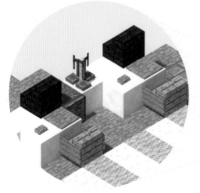

3 The observatory contains tanks made from ice blocks for mob specimen collection.

4 It's important to provide underwater spaces with natural air, so plants, trees and crops are a necessity. The materials they produce allow residents to be self-sufficient.

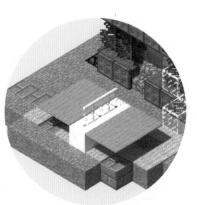

5 Activities under the ocean are limited. Installations like the pool table and table tennis area are necessary for keeping the inhabitants occupied.

STEAMPUNK AIRSHIP

Combining Victorian-era technology with sci-fi machinery, this steampunk airship may seem like an abnormality in terms of architecture, but the shapes, features and decoration share more similarities with regular builds than you would expect.

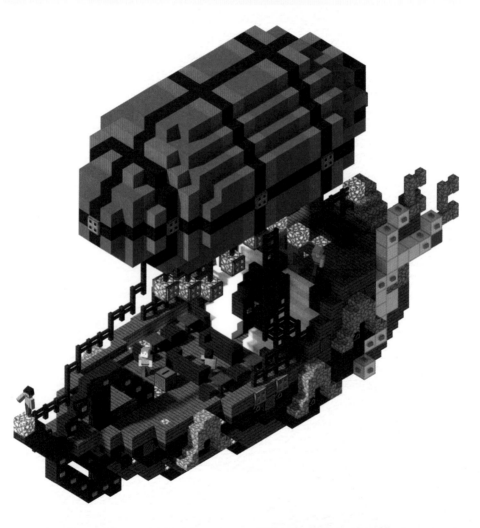

STEAMPUNK THEME

TRIADIC

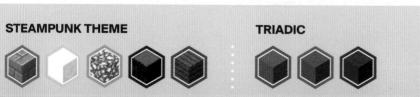

SCHEMATICS

The airship's balloon is an ovoid, or 3D oval. This is constructed in a similar way to a sphere, but the widest circle of the sphere is duplicated many times to elongate the shape. The deck is an irregular shape, but is similar to an upside-down triangular prism.

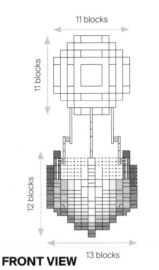

11 blocks

11 blocks

12 blocks

FRONT VIEW 13 blocks

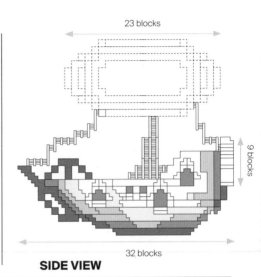

23 blocks

9 blocks

32 blocks

SIDE VIEW

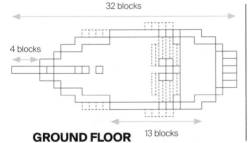

32 blocks

4 blocks

GROUND FLOOR 13 blocks

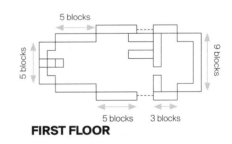

5 blocks

5 blocks

9 blocks

5 blocks   3 blocks

FIRST FLOOR

END CITY

IDEAL LANDSCAPE

The airship doesn't require any land, but you'll need to create foundations to begin building in the sky. It can be constructed in any biome, but a more fantastical landscape like the End city, with its unusual colours, crooked towers and floating pirate ships, suits the science fiction nature of this build.

STEAMPUNK AIRSHIP EXTERIOR

1 Gold is often used in steampunk-style constructs, so glowstone lends itself well to this build. Attach blocks to wooden fence posts hanging above the deck.

2 Cogs and clockwork mechanisms are characteristic of steampunk style. Solid blocks are used to create these on the hull, adding depth through decoration.

Other iconic steampunk features include mechanisms related to steam power, such as windmills, chimneys, water wheels and rudders. These add thematic decoration to the ship.

 Some common architectural features have been incorporated into this build. Roofed bay windows are dotted along the exterior of the hull, and short spires sit on top of some rooms.

STEAMPUNK AIRSHIP INTERIOR

1 Additional detail like levers, framed maps, banners and a grandfather clock complete the interior decoration and fit into the mechanistic style.

2 The galley contains everything required to feed the crew: ovens, fridges and plenty of seating for everyone.

3 An industrial-style floor made from sideways pistons makes a suitable steampunk grounding inside the hull of the ship.

The ship travels around collecting loot and trading, so there needs to be plenty of storage space. More functional decoration like shulker boxes and chests serve this purpose.

The engine room of the airship is filled with functional furnaces to make the steam that powers the airship.

FINAL WORDS

Congratulations! You've reached the end of our Guide to Creative! We hope you've been inspired to make something amazing.

One of the best things about Creative mode is that there's no right or wrong way to play. You set your own goals. Never feel disheartened when you see someone else's unbelievably epic creation. Remember that lots of the epic builds you might find on the internet have been worked on for months on end and constructed by large teams of experienced builders.

Having access to limitless resources can be intimidating too, but using most of the blocks on offer won't necessarily make your creations shine. It's more important to follow through on a vision, whether it's a monumental skyscraper that dominates the skyline or a modest forest home.

Enough reading! Get building!

OWEN JONES
THE MOJANG TEAM

STAY IN THE KNOW!

GUIDE TO: ☑CREATIVE

GUIDE TO: ☒EXPLORATION

GUIDE TO: ☐THE NETHER & THE END

GUIDE TO: ☐REDSTONE

MINECRAFT M@BESTIARY — AN ILLUSTRATED GUIDE TO THE MOBS OF MINECRAFT.

MINECRAFT MEDIEVAL FORTRESS — BUILDS

MINECRAFT — THE SURVIVORS' BOOK OF SECRETS

MINECRAFT THE ISLAND
NEW YORK TIMES BESTSELLER
MAX BROOKS
AUTHOR OF WORLD WAR Z

Learn about the latest Minecraft books
when you sign up for our newsletter at
RANDOMHOUSEBOOKS.COM/MINECRAFT

DEL REY

MOJANG